KT-592-829

The Country Life Picture Book of
The Cotswolds
and surrounding country

The Country Life Picture Book of
The Cotswolds
and surrounding country

Hugh Newbury

COUNTRY LIFE BOOKS

Frontispiece Owlpen Manor, Gloucestershire.

COUNTRY · LIFE

🛇🛇🛇🛇🛇🛇🛇🛇🛇

NEWNES·BOOKS

Published by Country Life Books
an imprint of Newnes Books
a Division of the Hamlyn Publishing Group Limited,
84/88 The Centre, Feltham, Middlesex, TW13 4BH
and distributed for them by
The Hamlyn Publishing Group Limited
Rushden, Northants, England

First published 1982
Second impression 1983

ISBN 0 600 36768 1

Set in 12/14 Bembo by
Photocomp Limited, Birmingham
Colour separations made by
Culver Graphics Litho Limited, High Wycombe
Printed in Italy

Introduction

I like to come to the Cotswolds from the west. You can perfectly well approach from any other direction, the landscape and the villages changing almost imperceptibly as you go. But I prefer the dramatic road from the west. Even before reaching Evesham you can see great cliffs marking the edge of the Cotswold escarpment jutting up from the Vale. Through Evesham, leaving behind the half-timbered houses, you begin to climb the hill and suddenly you are in Broadway, the most famous of all the Cotswold villages. From the top of the scarp, the Vale of Evesham is spread out behind you, with the Malvern Hills and Wales beyond, and ahead the Cotswolds themselves.

The Cotswold hills stretch from just south of Stratford-upon-Avon in a south-westerly direction almost to Bristol and Bath, a distance of about forty miles. From this scarp the land falls away to the south and east, and exactly where the Cotswolds end here is very much a matter of personal taste. Local purists will argue endlessly for or against including this place or that, but I do not think we need join their debate.

For the purposes of this book I have included not just the immediate Cotswold area, but also some of the towns and cities that stand guard round the edge, for the sake of the influence they seem to have had at various times throughout history on the affairs of the whole region. Indeed, the Cotswolds form part of the very 'Heart of England'.

First, perhaps, some facts. The underlying rock of the escarpment is that band of limestone that stretches from Yorkshire to Dorset, and the particular sort that forms the Cotswolds is called oolitic limestone. This consists of a mass of small spherical grains, the exact texture and colour varying with the location and depth. Being relatively soft, it has been moulded by wind and rain into a rolling countryside, with sudden ridges and small, steep-sided valleys cut by the streams that drain the hills. The highest point, the hill marvellously named Cleeve Cloud, is just over 1000ft, something the summer visitor easily forgets. If he returned in winter he would find the gentle holiday weather transformed—bitter winds to drive the rain and snow, confirmed by the local rhyme about 'Stow-on-the-Wold, where the wind blows cold'.

A dominant feature of the Cotswolds is its trees. Often they are beech, a natural inhabitant of a limestone country. Even today, when we are mourning the loss of so many trees, the Cotswolds give the appearance of having more than many parts of the country.

In prehistoric times most of southern Britain was thickly forested, and the early men, nomadic hunter-gatherers crossing the landbridge from Europe, soon discovered that it was easier to travel by way of the hilltops and ridges, more lightly wooded than the valleys with their dense undergrowth. These first people were followed by men who imported with them a whole new way of living: they were the first farmers.

From about 3500 BC these new immigrants brought livestock and seed corn and began a more settled existence in forest clearings. Gradually their way of life and their technology, including the shaping and firing of clay to make pottery cooking and storage vessels, spread among the original population of hunter-gatherers, but perhaps the most spectacular skill they brought was that of building monuments for their dead. Huge burial mounds were constructed in which a dozen or more remains have been found. Later tombs were made of enormous blocks of stone covered with a mound of earth—Hetty Pegler's Tump near Uley is an impressive example—and this kind of building culminated eventually in Stonehenge. Because the tracks and ridgeways of these people were on higher ground, their monuments are naturally found there too. The Cotswolds have the Rollright Stones, just north of Chipping Norton, their mysterious loneliness somehow emphasised by the presence of visitors.

With the coming first of a bronze technology (about 1800 BC) followed rather more than a millennium later by iron, man began to have an increasing effect on his environment: it is very much easier to make a forest clearing with an iron axe than with a stone one. More ambitious mining could now be attempted, and it was the rich mineral deposits, of gold, tin and lead, that attracted the Romans.

The Romans were marvellous administrators and had a profound and lasting influence on the land and the history of England. I have sometimes thought that it must be due to them that from the time of their invasion and conquest of this country our history can be tabulated neatly into 500-year chunks, thus:

    0– 500 The Romans
  500–1000 The Saxons and then the Danes
 1000–1500 The Normans and the Middle Ages
 1500–2000 Modern times

This division, although rather approximate (everyone knows it was really 1066, not 1000), is not entirely frivolous, since it points up the time scale quite neatly. Roman influence survived in England for a period equal to that between Henry VII and our own day.

Their administrators followed the troops everywhere, and so they came to Cirencester where they made their provincial capital and where three of their meticulously planned roads meet. Akeman Street goes off north-eastwards in the direction of Bedford. The Foss Way, running from Exeter to Lincoln, was originally a frontier way, in the days before the conquest of the western midlands. It was built just east of the Cotswold scarp, an ideal defensive line against disgruntled Britons in the Severn Valley, and one can see in the mind's eye the Roman sentry on the top of the scarp staring into the gloom and wondering whether the dawn would bring another attack. The third road at Cirencester, sometimes called the West Way, was their line of communication with Silchester and London, and it had been continued westwards to the fort guarding the river crossing at a place we call Gloucester.

As the pacification of the country proceeded in the first century AD there grew up an ordered social life among the increasing numbers of the well-to-do, based on the country house. From the standpoint of the troubled twentieth century it seems to have been an idyllic life: a beautiful peaceful countryside, fertile farms, plenty of labour from a docile local population (all problems ruthlessly solved by the militia) and, above all, the benefits of Roman technology about the house. The finest of the Cotswold villas must have been Chedworth, with its mosaics and its marvellous wooded setting.

But the withdrawal of the legions in the fifth century AD to help defend the Rhine frontier of the Empire left Britain open to attack and eventually colonisation by people from northern Germany. The Anglo-Saxon Chronicle paints a dark picture: cities sacked, the inhabitants killed.

In 571 AD 'Cuthulf fought with the Britons at Bedford and took four towns, Lenbury, Aylesbury, Benson and Ensham'—uncomfortably close to the Cotswolds. Then in 577 'Cuthwin and Ceawlin fought with the Britons and slew three kings, Commail and Condida and Farinmail, on the spot that is called Derham, and took from them three cities, Gloucester, Cirencester and Bath.'

The ordered life was at an end in the Cotswolds for the time being, but in a natural evolution the conquerors became settlers, the populations intermarried and country people found, as always, more pressing problems in their crops than in the politics and the skirmishings of their rulers.

During the next thousand years the harvest was often interrupted—by Norse and Breton raiders coming up the Severn, by men in the livery of one or another squabbling baron, and later by Cromwell's cavalry jingling down the lanes. And, between times, farming evolved too.

Sheep had been the mainstay of Cotswold life from the earliest times. The very name 'Cotswolds' comes from the Saxon and means 'the hills of the sheepfolds'. The Romans had found fuller's earth, used in one of the clothmaking processes, in the Cotswolds where it was later to be rediscovered. By the early Middle Ages fortunes were being discreetly made by the abbeys that owned much of the grazing land. At this time most of the wool, apart from what was needed locally, was 'exported' from the area, often to the Low Countries, and the middleman, the wool merchant, began to grow rich too. Indeed so rich did some of them become that they were the King's main source of finance for his wars. The wealth of the Church, however, tended to stay in its hands: the Norman-French lawyers coined the phrase 'mortmain' ('dead hand') for this grasp of land which, so the Church thought, it would hold in perpetuity. By contrast the wool merchants often put their money back into the Cotswolds, some of it, of course, into the great churches, as an afterlife insurance, but also, for their comfort in the meantime, into splendid houses. Fairford's magnificent church, for instance, was built in about 1500 by John Tame, and his son married into the Grevel (later Greville) family whose wool fortune had enabled them to build one of the loveliest houses in Chipping Campden.

Chipping Campden is the north Cotswold wool town *par excellence*. The High Street, where William Grevel built his house, seems to have fallen asleep at some long-past moment of such perfection that one can only stand and stare. It is not just the warmth of the stone and the steep lichen-covered roofs, with dormer windows and gables providing accents along the street. It is not even the feeling that, as in Cirencester, the architecture is on a truly human scale, so unlike that of a modern town. There is here a sense of 'the past continuing in the present': the spirit of Campden's heyday is strong enough still to survive in the late twentieth century.

The distribution of the monastic lands at the Reformation served to increase the numbers of landed gentry who were making money from sheep. Farming methods were slowly improving too: the old strip farming, although highly organised on a village basis, was inefficient in terms of cash returns. In the Cotswolds, as in other parts of the country where sheep predominated, there had always been a tendency to enclose land, and from the sixteenth century onwards this trend became more marked. Often hedges were used to enclose individual fields, but the readily available Cotswold stone made a barrier at once quicker to build and more impenetrable than a hedge. So the craft of dry-stone walling developed alongside those of the quarrier and the stonemason.

Another change that was taking place at this time was in the cloth trade. Previously most cloth had been made on the continent, but various economic and political factors, not least the influx of Protestant refugees with craft secrets, encouraged the home trade to expand. The spinning and weaving of wool, from being a cottage craft, in the late fifteenth century became a cottage industry. Whole families were employed by wool merchants to turn the local raw material into cloth, and the weavers' cottages, to us so rural in appearance, are in reality a part of our industrial heritage. Fuller's earth was rediscovered around Stroud, which became the centre of the new trade and a magnet for other cloth craftsmen, such as dyers.

For three centuries the Cotswold boom continued

Hidcote Manor, Gloucestershire, has one of the finest gardens in England.

in the villages straggling up the steep-sided valleys round Stroud. More and more money was invested in the trade and ways of speeding production sought. One way was not hard to spot: water power. The little valleys had fast-flowing rivers ideal for powering water mills, and in the eighteenth century the valleys below the weavers' cottages began to burgeon with factories, at first small, then increasingly large.

It is strange now to come upon one of these buildings in such a rural setting. But then these mills are not the 'dark satanic' ones of Blake. They are almost cosy factories, clean, light, perhaps slightly severe as befits such a serious enterprise as making money. But no belching smoke, no grime, no hiss and roar of steam: instead a cheerful stream and the sparkling Cotswold air.

The prosperity was not to last. The age of water power was a short interlude between the increasingly ousted craftsman and the factory hand. It has something of each, but mostly it was an interlude that was in truth industrial, the rural setting obliterated for the workpeople by the conditions inside the factories, the intolerably long hours, even for small children, and always the grinding poverty. By the end of the eighteenth century steam power in the north of England had taken the Industrial Revolution another step along the road, and the Cotswolds cloth trade evaporated. Some mills did convert to steam and persisted through most of the nineteenth century and even beyond: at Witney you can still buy the woollen blankets for which the town has been famous for centuries. But they were the exceptions. Those entrepreneurs who arrived on the scene late in the eighteenth century were just in time to lose their money.

The eighteenth century saw three other events that were to alter the landscape. The first was the agricultural revolution that preceded the industrial one. This involved two interlinked advances: the

Making a solid wall without mortar takes skill and patience. The craftsmen seem to have acquired a feeling for the raw material that amounts almost to empathy. Indeed finding the precise stone that will not merely lie snugly on the layer below but also help to bind the separate stones into a secure structure is no job for the beginner. Such craft is now rare and expensive, and electric fences are replacing dry-stone walls.

completion of the enclosures and a more scientific and technological approach to the whole business of farming. Better yields resulted from a different rotation of crops in the fields (first demonstrated on his Norfolk farm by that noble farmer beloved of English schoolboys, 'Turnip' Townshend). Sheep-breeding, too, was vastly improved.

The completion of the enclosures unfortunately caused great distress to countless people. The thousands of acres of open fields under the old strip farming system were redivided into more efficient farms with fields enclosed by hedges or walls. But people whose families had for generations been farming the same strips under the protection of village custom were faced with having to prove a legal right to their share or lose their livelihood and their homes. It was the end of the peasant economy, when every village household had a few small parcels of land to farm in the open field and the right to graze animals and to collect fuel on the waste or common land, much of which was now also enclosed and ploughed. The effects were a sudden migration of poor people from the land into the towns, with their new industries, and in the country the beginnings of an efficient mechanised agriculture that was to become increasingly industrial. Oliver Goldsmith wrote his *Deserted Village* with just these conditions in mind:

Ill fares the land, to hast'ning ills a prey,
Where wealth accumulates and men decay;
Princes and lords may flourish, or may fade—
A breath can make them, as a breath has
    made—
But a bold peasantry, their country's pride,
When once destroy'd can never be supplied.

The second innovation in the eighteenth century was the canal. The Duke of Bridgwater built the first in 1761 (the first modern one, that is: the Romans, who managed to do almost everything centuries before everyone else, built a canal, the Fossdyke, still in use, to link the Witham and the Trent in Lincolnshire). For the next seventy years canals were the chief means of transport for heavy goods, at something like half the cost of road transport. Stroud had a canal running from the Severn to the Thames at Lechlade, which brought coal to the steam-powered mills trying to compete with the northern ones.

A third eighteenth-century development was tourism. It was the century of the Grand Tour, when a youth and his tutor would pass an expensive and flea-bitten few months travelling in the safer (or sometimes, by mistake, in the more dangerous) parts of Europe. Their elders travelled as well. Dr Johnson, an indefatigable voyager (he planned an abortive trip to Italy at the age of 75), clambered round the highlands and islands of Scotland with Boswell, and even spent a month or so in Paris where, his spoken French not being of the best, he addressed the natives in vigorous and fluent Latin.

At home it was the thing to go at the proper time to Bath, to take the waters and to meet one's friends. Cheltenham was a small market town when in 1716 a farmer was fortunate enough to find a saline spring. The local businessmen did not have to be very astute to see in their town a rival for Bath that, with luck, might make them rich. And so it proved. In time, and particularly after the visit by George III in 1788, it became the eighteenth-century equivalent of a health farm where, as Cobbett caustically wrote:

East India plunderers, West India floggers, English tax-gorgers, together with gluttons, drunkards and debauchees forgather at the suggestion of silently laughing quacks, in the hope of getting rid of the bodily consequences of their manifold sins and iniquities.

The town of Cheltenham provides the visitor an

agreeable 'day off' from the rustic stone architecture and haphazard plan of the typical Cotswold town. Here we find a sophisticated and elegant city, clearly designed and built to please the highest Society. The dominant architectural style is Greek, but with refreshing excursions into the Italian Renaissance as well. The mixture is wholly charming, partly because the town planning, with broad streets, long vistas and carefully placed open spaces, is generous and allows individual buildings to be seen to the best advantage while at the same time making sure they contribute to the total effect.

Stratford-upon-Avon too began to attract its share of visitors in the eighteenth century. In September 1769 there was a 'Jubilee', the first ever held, to celebrate Stratford's cult figure. The prime mover was David Garrick, who as the best-known actor-manager of the day had a vested interest in the Bard. An amphitheatre was built and, we are told, 'every Species of Entertainment was exhibited; such as Concerts, Oratorios, Pageants, Fireworks, Illuminations, &c.' Is it possible there was no performance of a Shakespeare play during the three days of the Jubilee? If so it was a real case of *Hamlet* without the Prince.

Stratford has since become the greatest tourist attraction in the country, and the effect on the Cotswolds has been enormous. To be on the coach route between London and Stratford must be like living in the forecourt of Buckingham Palace. But Stratford itself is quite accustomed to its daily invasion and acts like a well-organised hostess. It has come to terms with the tourist and, indeed, leads a busy life of its own. The cattle market is a serious weekly affair, and a visitor to the town in October might be forgiven for being seduced from his Shakespearean studies by the annual junketing of the Mop Fair which has been held since long before Shakespeare's time.

On the eastern rim of the Cotswolds, Oxford too has its own life to lead, a life from which the visitor feels more excluded than in almost any other town. Here, one feels, there is no pretending: in Oxford one is no more than a tourist.

Oxford is the country's senior university (and in Europe second only to the Sorbonne), but its main connection with and influence on the Cotswolds lies in its position during the Civil War as the Royalist headquarters and seat of the Royal Parliament. Many of the colleges followed the example of the loyal families of the well-to-do in melting down their silver to help the cause of Charles I. The whole area between Oxford and Gloucester was fought over, the struggle taking the form of skirmishes on a local scale and of sieges of a manor house or castle to oust or capture a particular influential supporter of one side or the other. It must have been a wretched time for the ordinary people, unable to prevent the destruction of their homes and the commandeering of their beasts and crops by sullen vanquished and boisterous victors alike. The fit young, and not so young, men had in any case been conscripted by their lord to fight and die with him on the wooded slopes of Edgehill or, in a downpour of rain, at the sack of Worcester.

There is a Cotswold connection with Oxford in Exeter College, for the Victorian chapel contains tapestries by William Morris who lived at Kelmscott, not far from Lechlade. With Burne-Jones, whose tapestries can also be seen in Exeter College chapel, Morris founded the Pre-Raphaelite Brotherhood which tried to combat the increasing mechanisation and general bad taste of much nineteenth-century art by insisting on the right of the individual craftsman to a say in the design of the product he was making. Mass-production spelled uniformity and the subservience of man to machine, and it may be that Morris was influenced in his choice of the Cotswolds by the thought of the local craftsmen-weavers of the Middle Ages. At any rate

Tewkesbury had a monastic community in the eighth century, but it was the Benedictines who built this magnificent abbey in the decades around 1100. The monastery buildings, including a Lady Chapel at the East End, were demolished on the orders of Henry VIII's commissioners in the 1540s. But six of the original chapels forming the chevet, three of whose roofs can be seen in the picture, still survive, giving the abbey an unusual continental look.

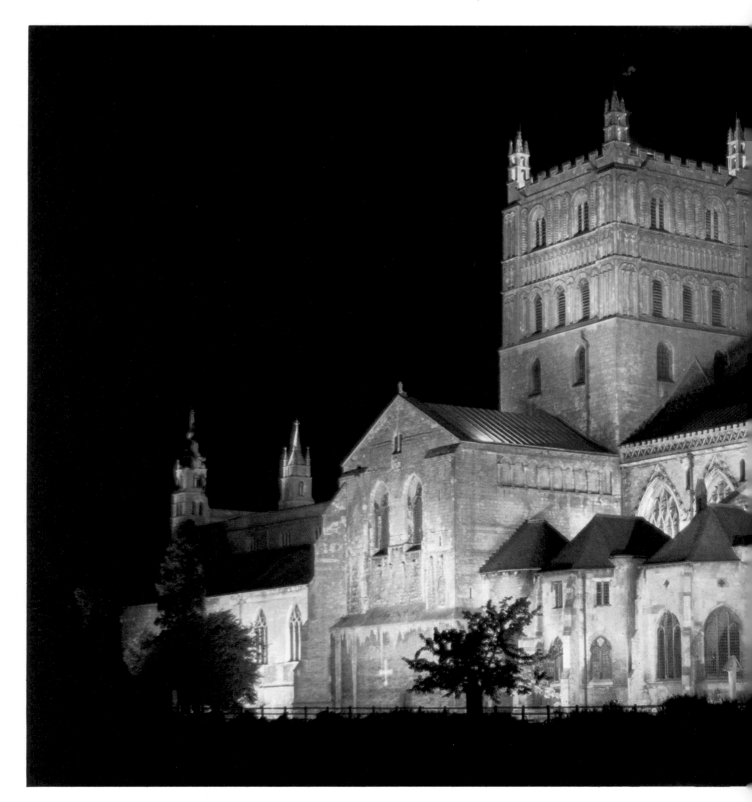

he had a profound influence on English design in many apparently unconnected fields, for it was part of the philosophy that all the different objects in a house should be designed to contribute to a harmonious whole. In 1861 he founded Morris & Co. to produce wallpapers, furniture, tapestries, stained glass windows, carpets and furnishing materials in a restrained style.

His anti-industrial theories were the cornerstone of the Arts and Crafts movement which did much to ensure a high standard of design against which the mass-produced objects could be measured.

He had another lasting effect: he started the 'Cotswold cult', the romantic notion of an ideal rustic world where life was uncomplicated by modernity and where the craftsman, the intellectual, the independent peasant farmer, the honest artisan could gain recognition, a livelihood, the satisfaction of handicraft as opposed to the drudgery of machine-minding.

The lunatic fringe took to it as well: the Distributionists, a dotty political group with which G. K. Chesterton was involved, proposed to solve England's problems by giving everyone 'two acres and a cow'.

More productively, William Morris's ideas had some direct descendants in the work of a group of furniture makers who became known as the Cotswold School. Ernest Gimson, a London architect, with the Barnsley brothers, Sydney and Ernest, moved to the Cotswolds in 1893, just before Morris's death. They set up a workshop first at Ween, near Cirencester, which they moved the next year to Pinbury and finally, in 1903, to Daneway, Gimson's house in Sapperton. The philosophy of the workshop was very much that of the Arts and Crafts movement. The designs were simple and vernacular, and the pieces were superbly made in the best traditions of rural English craftsmanship.

After the First World War, another influential furniture designer, Gordon Russell (later Sir

Gordon), established a workshop in Broadway, following very much the same principles. It was in operation through the 1920s and 1930s. In the Second World War, Russell was asked to produce designs for a 'Utility' range of furniture to be mass-produced on a huge scale—an ironic full turn of the wheel.

More ordinary people began to feel a romantic nostalgia for the countryside. (Perhaps the English had always had this attachment to the country rather than to the town. Gordon Winter, in *The Country Life Picture Book of Britain*, pointed out that English culture is country-based: William Morris may just have been reminding the Victorians of a half-forgotten but enduring facet of the English character.)

This has led to a whole fashion for things rural, from the 'second home'—complete with fitted kitchen in 'stripped pine' veneer—to an enormous increase in holiday travel in the Cotswolds and similar country areas.

Indeed, tourism, since those beginnings at Cheltenham in the eighteenth century, has grown until, as an industry, it rivals agriculture. This growth has led to some conflict of interest, and it is significant that Gloucestershire County Council has an officer whose job it is to make sure that visitors have as much access to the countryside as possible while at the same time causing the least disruption to farming and other local interests. There are dozens of groups engaged in promoting one or another aspect of conservation, ranging from the Royal Society for the Protection of Birds to the Society for the Protection of Rural England. It is a typically haphazard English situation that nevertheless actually works in the Cotswolds because the people involved are determined that it shall. Difficulties are solved by discussion between personal friends, and disputes are rare.

Certainly the visitor finds few problems; even the thousands of tourists do not seem to obtrude very much. It is a curious fact that the huge open spaces of the Scottish Highlands seem more crowded than the Cotswolds. This may be because in Western Scotland there is generally only one road in an area that everyone must use. The delight of the Cotswolds is that there is a network of little lanes leading through an almost deserted countryside to tiny villages seemingly quite innocent of the tourist trade. If conservationists can maintain this happy state of affairs, residents and visitors alike will be thankful.

In 1380 William Grevel, 'the flower of the wool merchants of all England', built himself a house in Chipping Campden, at the upper end of the High Street, where he died in 1401. It is still, wrote G. M. Trevelyan in *English Social History*, 'an ornament of the most beautiful village street now left in the island'. He was one of the first Cotswold capitalists and, after the custom of the time, used his wealth to benefit his town, particularly the great wool church.

But it was Sir Baptist Hicks, in the early seventeenth century, who perhaps more than anyone else left his mark on Campden. Though the house he built for himself was destroyed in the Civil War (by drunken Royalists, it is said), his almshouses are still there, and so is his famous Market Hall. The quaintly elegant look of the outside (*above*) does not prepare one for the massive workaday interior (*right*), with its arching beams and rough stone floor.

19

Conservationists say that burning stubble fields after the harvest (*below*) destroys habitats. People with horses bemoan the straw, left by modern combine harvesters, that also gets burnt. Farmers know that the yield in the year following burning is considerably increased because the fire destroys weed seeds and insect pests with their eggs, and generally cleans the soil surface. There can be no single right answer to such arguments.

Dover Hill near Campden (*left*), now owned by the National Trust, was for two hundred years the scene of the amazing Cotswold Games. They were founded in the seventeenth century by a local lawyer named Robert Dover and were called the 'Olympicks', though some of the events would have alarmed the ancient Greeks. They would no doubt have enjoyed the horseracing, wrestling and dancing, and might have coped with the coursing and cockfighting; but what of the shin-kicking contest? Rowdy scenes put a stop to the Games in 1851, and no wonder. Recently, however, they have been revived, and a popular item is always the 'battle' according to seventeenth-century rules, performed, if that is the right word, by the Sealed Knot Society.

Apple-blossom time in the Vale of Evesham.

Peace . . .

Until 1928 the Four Shire Stone stood at the point where Gloucestershire, Worcestershire, Warwickshire and Oxfordshire all met. Worcestershire's boundary was then moved away, but no one has the heart to demote the stone.

If Chipping Campden has the most beautiful village street in England, then Broadway must surely have the most famous one. The picture postcard effect is largely due to the spectacular cottage gardens that line the streets. The colours, nowhere more riotous than here, are enhanced by the quiet gold of the stone, and on any day of the year you care to mention the whole scene attracts as many visitors, seemingly, as a football match.

Broadway is built under the edge of the Cotswold scarp, which rises sharply behind the village, and the view from the top, across the Vale of Evesham towards the Malvern Hills and Wales, is magnificent. An eighteenth-century Earl of Coventry built Broadway Tower, at the request of his wife, who had wondered whether the hill could be seen from their house near Worcester. Rossetti, Burne-Jones and William Morris were early holidaymakers here.

A few miles from Broadway, Stanton seems to have escaped the rush of tourists by being just off the main road. It is, if possible, even more idyllic and is marvellously cared for, like all the Cotswold villages. But Stanton had the advantage of having, as lord of the manor for many years, the architect Philip Stott, who planned and supervised the upkeep and restoration of the buildings, most of which date from the sixteenth and seventeenth centuries.

The next village to Stanton on the same byroad is Stanway. Its name comes from the Stane Way, the old road up the Cotswold scarp, and its chief delights are Stanway House, built by the Tracy family, its medieval tithe barn and this Jacobean gateway, built in about 1630, but not by Inigo Jones as is sometimes said. It bears the arms of John Tracy impaling those of Atkyns, his wife's family, which were no doubt added at their marriage in 1701.

From Stanton (*see page 30*) one can climb the ridge
behind the village and look down on Snowshill. The
manor here, looked after by the National Trust, was
built in about 1500 and boasts this jack in the form
of a solemn St George, concentrating on the need to
slay the dragon at his feet while at the same time
striking the bell suspended over his head. The
church was rebuilt in the 1860s with a rather squat
massiveness and more or less in a style of some six
centuries earlier. But the village street has the
traditional Cotswold cottages, the warm stone and
white paint setting off the flowers in the little
gardens to perfection.

Water, lush vegetation and Cotswold stone seem to
go hand in hand.

Timber-framed houses are uncommon on the
Cotswold escarpment itself, where stone is the main
building material. To the north and west, on the
other hand, there are plenty. This house (*right*) at
Didbrook, not far from Winchcombe, is on the
boundary between the two areas and so is a mixture
of them both. The gable consists of two massive
timbers in the shape of an inverted V, with other
timbers supporting them. This type of construction
is known as a cruck. The filling between the timbers
was originally of wattle and daub (twigs and small
branches covered with a layer of mud or clay), but
later brick or, as here, stone was used. This cottage
may date from as long ago as the fifteenth century.

Sudeley Castle, seen on the right of the picture below basking in the sunshine, has many royal connections, not least with Katherine Parr who, having contrived to outlive Henry VIII, married Admiral Lord Seymour, the owner of the castle, where in 1548 she died in childbirth and where she is buried. Most visitors enjoy venturing back into history in the quiet gardens, but for some the attraction may be the chomp and hiss of steam engines at the annual Steam Fair.

Winchcombe, a short way from Sudeley, was once the centre of Winchcombeshire. It acquired this status as a royal manor in about 1000 AD and kept it for some twenty years, when it was merged with Gloucestershire. These ancient stocks (*opposite, bottom*) stand outside the Town Hall. The church of St Peter is one of the great wool churches of the county, with a nave built by Sir Ralph Boteler, the builder of Sudeley. It is decorated with a marvellous series of grotesque heads (*below*).

In today's Cotswolds, as for a thousand years, sheep
may safely graze . . .

Stow-on-the-Wold, has a very large market square, reflecting its position as one of the major commercial centres of the medieval Cotswolds. The ancient cross now has a top added by the Victorians, who also gave Stow St Edward's Hall, with its spire.

Autumn in Upper Slaughter.

Lower Slaughter meanders picturesquely beside a brook crossed at suitable intervals by little bridges. At the upper end of the village the stream has been put to work: a brick-built mill, rather self-consciously industrial-looking beside the stone cottages, was constructed in the early nineteenth century to grind corn. Its water-wheel is still in place. But picturesqueness won: millstones now help the spring flowers to decorate cottage gardens.

Near the villages of Guiting Power and Temple
Guiting is the Cotswold Farm Park, where rare
breeds of farm animals are preserved. Of course the
sheep, such as this splendidly horned Jacob ram, are
here, but so too are pigs, cattle and even reindeer.
Perhaps even more crucial than just keeping breeds
alive is the attempted re-creation by cross-breeding
of ones that have already disappeared, so as to
establish a unique gene-bank for livestock breeders.

The walls of this house in Lower Slaughter (*opposite*)
are made of 'courses' or layers of stones of different
thicknesses, making a pleasing decorative effect.

Baling straw under a late summer sky.

The 'Water' of Bourton-on-the-Water is the River Windrush, a broad stream running through the town flanked by expanses of grass (*see page 48*). It must be one of the most attractive small towns anywhere in England, and indeed it gets its fair share of tourists, for whom it caters with an aquarium, a breeding collection of butterflies, a park with 600 species of birds and a large model railway. But the best-known attraction is the model village (actually Bourton itself) constructed to a one-ninth scale. The detail is amazingly good: only the flowers (and of course the visitors) give the game away.

The Romans built what was probably the first
bridge across the Windrush when they were
constructing the Fosse Way. In the centuries that
followed several others have been built, forming
one of the features of Bourton that visitors most
remember.

In Bourton even pottery mantel dogs take to the
windows to enjoy the view.

It is good to find old farm equipment, such as this
wagon, being preserved instead of being allowed to
rot away. Industrial archaeology covers
agriculture too.

It was Nash who saw that the terrace, with its imposing façade, divided into separate residences, would give the owner (and, more important, his friends) the impression that he was living in a palace. The Regent's Park terraces in London are perhaps a shade pompous: here at Cheltenham (*opposite, bottom*) there is a lightness and grace that make them rather more welcoming.

Classical details abound. The Pittville Pump Room (*left*) has a colonnade based on that of a temple in Athens, though the builder used a lovely warm Cotswold stone in place of the brilliant marble of the original. Not far away these caryatids, sisters of the ones in the Erechtheum on the Acropolis, elegantly support a row of shop-fronts.

The Devil's Chimney (*below*), just outside
Cheltenham.

Yanworth (*right*) is remarkable for the Norman
church unusually situated in a farmyard. One can
also see this attractively flower-decked wall.

This mosaic (*above*) is in Chedworth Roman Villa, beautifully set in a wooded valley not far from the Fosse Way. It was built round two courtyards and had two bath suites: one a Turkish bath, the other a sauna. The building dates from the second century AD. The site has a long history of occupation: close by are a large Bronze Age round barrow and a Roman temple.

This Norman gatehouse of about 1180 *(top)* is all
that remains of Cirencester's Augustinian abbey.

Swans decorate the River Churn at Cirencester.

In Roman times Cirencester *(opposite)*, then called
Corinium Dobunnorum, was the largest town in
Britain after London. It was a vital frontier garrison
town in the Roman drive west from the relatively
safe base in south-east England, and the

meeting place of the main roads the Romans used
for the rapid dissemination of news and, if necessary,
troops. Its position ensured the continued prosperity
of Cirencester which, with the great Augustinian
abbey and the wealth brought by the wool trade,
gave it the title of 'the capital of the Cotswolds'. The
parish church of St John the Baptist (*below*) must be
one of the largest and most elaborate in the country.
The south porch dates from 1490.

The Great Hall of Berkeley Castle.

Berkeley Castle is one of the oldest inhabited castles in Britain, having been the home of the Berkeley family since 1153. The most famous event in its long history (and without doubt the grimmest) was the particularly brutal murder here in 1327 of Edward II. The moated castle stares balefully out over the flat Vale of Berkeley towards the Severn estuary, and it is not hard to imagine, in its heyday, the oppressiveness of the massive battlements bearing down on the surrounding countryside—or the reassurance of its presence, depending on your allegiance. Today's visitors, after the sinister thrills of the castle itself, can walk in the sunny gardens and admire the trees and the shrubs and the water lilies. Incidentally, Edward Jenner, the inventor of vaccination, was the doctor at Berkeley and first tried out his ideas on the trusting local people.

Tetbury lies towards the southern end of the
Cotswolds, a pleasant market town of broad streets
and sudden steep places. The Market Place is the hub
of the town and has an interesting seventeenth-
century Market House supported on columns.
Tetbury was one of the chief centres of the medieval
wool trade: merchants' houses can be found in the
streets off the Market Place, and the market itself
was still important in the nineteenth century.

Westonbirt Arboretum is one of the glories of the
region and should on no account be missed by
anyone with the slightest interest in trees.
Westonbirt House, now a girls' school, was built in
the 1860s by Lewis Vulliamy for R. S. Holford,
whose chief passion was gardening and particularly
the cultivation of trees. He started the Arboretum
which, now run by the Forestry Commission, has
been considerably enlarged until it covers well over
100 acres. It is said that virtually every tree that can
be grown in the open in this part of the country
may be found in the gardens. It is at its most
colourful in spring, or, as here, in autumn.

To most people the name 'Badminton' means only
one thing: horses. Badminton House has been the
home of the Dukes of Beaufort since
Elizabethan times, and the passion of the Somersets
(the family name) for hunting goes back further still.
But it was not until the mid 1700s that the fifth duke
brought foxhunting to the county, and there have
been hounds at Badminton ever since. The
popularity of hunting there can be judged from this
large field.

But if hunting is relatively a minority sport, the
same cannot be said for the Badminton Horse Trials.
For hundreds of thousands of visitors it is a fixed
point in the April calendar, and they travel long
distances to see the top riders and their horses
perform. The three phases are the dressage, the
cross-country and the show-jumping, where only
the best can do well and even the best can fail.

In 1946 the Wildfowl Trust set up a research station on reclaimed land beside the Severn. Now thousands of ducks, geese (these are Greater Snow Geese) and swans, knowing they will be welcome, come here each year to breed. Slimbridge is famous throughout the world; in addition to being able to get close to the 180 species of birds, visitors can enjoy the permanent exhibitions including free films.

A huge Roman villa with over sixty rooms was discovered at Woodchester in the eighteenth century. The main hall has a beautiful mosaic floor depicting the story of Orpheus charming the animals with his lute. The floor (*below*) is kept covered over, but every few years it is uncovered for inspection by conservation experts and the public.

One of a chain of five picturesque lakes in Woodchester Park (*opposite*).

Unlikely as it might seem, this peaceful valley was once deeply involved in the thrust and vigour of the Industrial Revolution. For this is Chalford in the Golden Valley of the River Frome. In the late eighteenth century the river and road were suddenly joined by a canal from the great waterway of the Severn, and coal and cloth passed along the valley and through a two-mile tunnel near Sapperton to reach the Thames at Lechlade. At about the same time cloth mills were built in the valley bottom to make use of the free power of the river. At the top of the steep slope the mill owners built their houses, with between them the huddle of weavers' cottages. The prosperity lasted only two or three decades into the nineteenth century: the tide of the Industrial Revolution, now at the flood in Lancashire, was ebbing in the Cotswolds. Fortunately the receding waters did not leave the Golden Valley an industrial wasteland: the cloth trade does not create tips and slagheaps. Indeed the small scale of the industry has bequeathed us a number of buildings ideally suited for today's craftsmen —potters, silversmiths, print-makers —often working as a community. This too, with the example of Kelmscott and the Broadway furniture-makers to follow, is now something of a Cotswold tradition.

Prinknash Abbey must be unique. The house goes
back to a hunting lodge that belonged to the abbot
of Gloucester. From the Dissolution of the
Monasteries it was in private hands for four
centuries until, in 1928, it was presented to the
Benedictines of Caldey. Thus a Catholic property
has been restored to Catholic ownership. Plans for a
Neo-Gothic church and cloister were modified in
favour of a stone building in a somewhat severe
modern style.

Winter near Cranham.

It is sometimes forgotten that Gloucester is quite a considerable port. This is made possible by the Gloucester and Berkeley Ship Canal (*see pages 74–75*) which joins the Severn estuary at Sharpness. These fine warehouses (*opposite*) date from the early part of the nineteenth century.

The massive circular piers in the nave of Gloucester cathedral (*left*) are Norman and are much taller than such columns generally are. The effect is exaggerated by the stunted triforium above. The choir, a most marvellous and very early example of the Perpendicular style, was begun about 1337, ten years after the murder of Edward II in nearby Berkeley Castle. The dates are no coincidence: the king's body in its ornate tomb in the north ambulatory of the cathedral drew such crowds of medieval tourists that an extensive programme of new building, including the fan-vaulted cloisters, was easily financed from their contributions.

Old Father Time (*below*) leads an international group of bell-ringers: (*left to right*) Ireland, England, Scotland and Wales.

Gloucester cathedral sparkling in the winter   sunshine.

Saving canals from being destroyed by neglect is one of the most laudable initiatives of preservation societies and other groups of enthusiasts. Luckily some canals are in constant commercial use and need no conservation, though cash for maintenance is always a problem. The Gloucester and Berkeley Ship Canal takes sizeable ships the sixteen miles between the deep water of the Severn estuary at Sharpness and the docks at Gloucester.

Another, lonelier, wetter use for the canal . . .

The seventeenth-century house of Westbury Court
has been demolished, but the National Trust are now
caring for the unique formal water garden (*opposite*)
dating from about 1700, the earliest in England.

The Severn road bridge (*below*) makes a graceful
trajectory across the wide river.

The Severn's horseshoe bend (*bottom*) seen from
Littledean.

Straw left behind in neat rows by the combine
harvester waits to be picked up — or burnt.

Watermills such as this one near Hartpury were once a common enough sight in the Severn valley, where there was plenty of power available. But small-scale mills were in the end overtaken by the urgent need to feed the growing masses in the industrial towns of the Midlands and North and, like much else from pre-industrial England, could not compete with the new steam-powered technology. Now we are having to rediscover and preserve their old technology.

In the Middle Ages the Church was supported to a considerable extent by tithes, a tax of one-tenth levied on agricultural produce, payable in kind. It was often resented by the peasant farmers, so that the Church had to take decisive steps to prevent the produce being 'borrowed back' by the local people. Hence tithe barns, such as this fine one at Ashleworth. The double doors allowed a wagon piled high with corn or hay to be driven right inside.

In the nineteenth century several Saxon churches were discovered which, probably since the Middle Ages, had been in constant use as ordinary domestic buildings. Bradwell-on-Sea was a barn, Bradford-on-Avon was a cottage with school attached, while this church (*right*), Odda's Chapel at Deerhurst, was (and still is) part of a medieval farmhouse. The nave, in the foreground, was the kitchen, and the chancel, seen through the arch, had been given an extra floor to provide an upstairs bedroom. Earl Odda was a kinsman of Edward the Confessor, and his chapel was dedicated in 1056. Not far away is one of the major Saxon monuments in the country, the church of St Mary, dating from about 800 AD.

This church at Upleadon is unusual in having a fine
half-timbered sixteenth-century tower.

The church of St Mary at Hill Croome (*opposite*)
dates from the late thirteenth century. The pulpit
has a tester, a sort of canopy, above it. This is not, as
is sometimes thought, just for decoration but to act
as a sounding board (which it is also called) to reflect
the preacher's voice down into the body
of the church and prevent it getting lost
in the vaulting.

Building a huge tithe barn, such as the one above at
Bredon, on the River Avon, was very much a
matter for professionals, and what a marvellous job
they made of it. The timbers, which may have lasted
now for as long as seven or eight hundred years (in
one Saxon church the timbers have been shown to
be 1000 years old), were often installed green, an
allowance being made in the structure for shrinkage
as the wood dried. All the timbers were sawn and
shaped elsewhere before being brought to the site
and erected, much like modern buildings
constructed by fitting together factory-made
sections.

Off the Cotswold escarpment to the north and west the older houses are often of half-timbered instead of stone construction, reflecting the differing availability of building materials. This one, at the village of Elmley Castle, is partly of brick, partly of stone and partly half-timbered. The village is one of a number sheltering under the lee of Bredon Hill which juts aggressively up out of the gentle Vale of Evesham. This is the country of the Archers, the farming family in the long-running BBC radio serial: another Bredon village, Ashton under Hill, is the model for the programme's fictitious Ambridge.

This view of Worcester cathedral gives one a comfortable picture of the city. The protective bulk of the great church seems to be acting the role of mother-hen to the brood of buildings huddled round. It conceals the devastation wrought by a generation of ruthless planners elsewhere in the city and the insensitivity of those responsible for the design of much of the centre of Worcester since the war. Charles II was defeated here by Cromwell in 1651.

The Avoncroft Museum of Buildings must be
unique in having as its main aim the preservation,
not the collecting, of exhibits. Only where it proves
impossible to prevent the destruction of a building
on its original site does the museum 'collect' it—in
the most literal way by dismantling it and
reassembling it at the open-air site at Stoke Heath.
The result is a fascinating exhibition of old buildings
that one can walk round and examine at one's
leisure, ranging from a working windmill and a
fifteenth-century merchant's house to this superb
thatched barn and the granary on its brick columns.
The museum is a registered charity.

The Severn Valley Railway runs for some thirteen miles between Bewdley and Bridgnorth and is one of the most important preserved railways in the country. Here an afternoon train from Bridgnorth arrives, puffing nostalgically, at Arley.

Lord Leycester's Hospital, Warwick.

An ancient signpost helpfully directs the traveller to
Warwick or to 'Woster'.

This dreamy view of Warwick Castle on a soft summer evening belies its warlike past. The oldest part was built soon after the Norman Conquest, but the castle was sacked by Simon de Montfort in 1264, and most of the present castle was built in the following two centuries. However fortune favoured the defenders in the Civil War, when the Parliamentarians successfully resisted a Royalist siege. Much of the castle was gutted in a fire in 1871.

It is almost easier to count the kings and queens who did not visit Kenilworth Castle, from Henry I onwards. Probably the most famous of all royal visits was in 1575 when Queen Elizabeth was entertained here by her favourite, the Earl of Leicester. The account by Sir Walter Scott is a considerably embroidered version of the truth, but one contemporary noted that the castle clock was stopped while the Queen was there, as a sign of welcome.

Ragley Hall, home of the Marquess of Hertford, was
built by Robert Hooke in about 1680. This is the
Prince Regent's bedroom. The 4th Marquess, a man
who fortunately combined prodigious wealth with
considerable taste, lived much of his life in Paris
where he put together a huge collection of
magnificent eighteenth-century French furniture
and works of art of all kinds. The collection passed
via his illegitimate son, Sir Richard Wallace, to the
nation in 1890, and is now on view in Wallace's
London home, Hertford House in Manchester
Square, under the name of the Wallace Collection.

Spring at Stratford-upon-Avon (*opposite*).

Charlecote Park (*below*) where Shakespeare is
alleged to have been caught stealing deer. He later
caricatured Charlecote's owner, Sir Thomas Lacy, as
Shallow, the country justice in *Henry IV*, part II,
and in *The Merry Wives of Windsor*.

The home at Wilmcote (*bottom*) of Mary Arden,
Shakespeare's mother.

The upkeep and restoration of old buildings is a constant task, and skilled stonemasons, like the one above in Stratford, are always in demand.

In the Bancroft Gardens, Stratford, is the Memorial by the Victorian sculptor Lord Ronald Gower. The four statues round it represent Tragedy, Comedy, Philosophy and, seen opposite, History in the form of Prince Hal.

The garden of Shakespeare's Birthplace (*opposite*) is devoted to the flowers and trees that occur in his works. Inside the sixteenth-century house the rooms have been provided with furniture of the period, and there is a museum with, among other exhibits, early editions of the plays.

Stoneleigh Abbey, seen below from across the park, started life in the middle of the twelfth century as a Cistercian monastery, of which a later gatehouse and one or two other fragments remain. Henry VIII gave the abbey to the Duke of Suffolk who in 1568 sold it to the Lord Mayor of London, Sir Thomas Leigh, in whose family it has remained ever since.

If Cheltenham is, so to speak, the child of George III, Leamington Spa is very much the creation of Victoria, who came here on a visit with her mother, the Duchess of Kent, in 1830, before she became Queen. The difference can somehow be felt in the two towns. Cheltenham is full of a leisured classical air that is wholly Georgian and Regency, while Leamington has that distinctly busier mid-Victorian charm characteristic of a successful nineteenth-century resort. The saline waters were found here as long ago as the sixteenth century, but it was not until 1814 that the first Pump Room was built near the Jephson Gardens (*right*), named after Dr Henry Jephson, the town's pioneer.

This remarkable classical windmill at Chesterton (*below*)
was built for Sir Edward Peyto in the 1630s as a lookout
point. Since the house, now long gone, was
designed by Inigo Jones, it is possible that the windmill was too.

Thatching (*opposite, top*) is a necessary country skill
even now.

Classical Farnborough Hall (*opposite, bottom*), a
National Trust property.

A newly gilded weathercock keeps watch over
wintry Charlbury.

The unbelievably beautiful Compton Wynyates
(*below*), home of the Marquis of Northampton. A
very early Tudor house, it was begun in the 1480s
and is built of a splendidly warm brick. The
romantic effect of the building itself, with its stone
mullioned windows and tall, apparently random,
chimneys, is enhanced by the ancient topiary garden
and the magic of the setting. The little church was
built after the Restoration in 1660 to replace the one
destroyed in the Civil War.

The Rollright Stones (*opposite*), not far from the
village of Great Rollright, a rough circle of over
seventy stones of varying size and shape, are thought
to date from the Bronze Age which began about
1800 BC. Perhaps they were the site of some
prehistoric ritual — indeed there was until
fairly recently a local custom involving the
elderbushes around the stones in a midsummer
ceremony that seems to have clear links with pre-
Christian religion. But this is a notoriously elusive
aspect of prehistory.

Broughton Castle, a fourteenth-century moated manor house.

The forecourt of Blenheim Palace on a misty
hunting morning.

The Baroque garden front of Blenheim (*opposite,
top*) overlooks a formal terrace with classical urns
and statuary intermingled with topiary. The palace
was a grateful nation's gesture of thanks to the Duke
of Marlborough, for which £500,000 was voted by
Parliament. Vanbrugh drew grand designs, but
delays, mounting costs, lack of supervision and sheer
extravagance produced, as they do today, endless
intractable problems.

The beautiful ironwork of the main entrance.

No doubt many of the Cotswolds' sheep spend
puzzling and anxious hours waiting in markets like
the one opposite.

This well-stocked Oxford shop would certainly sell
trout from one of the Cotswold trout farms.

Christ Church (*bottom*), generally referred to colloquially as 'the House', was founded in 1524 by Cardinal Wolsey. Tom Tower is the original gateway to the college, but the upper part was added by Sir Christopher Wren in 1682. It houses a large bell known as Great Tom.

Bicycles wait on the cobbles with the choirboys, whose medieval dress does not extend as far as their warm stockings and sensible shoes.

All Souls College was founded in 1437 by Archbishop Chichele to provide masses for the souls of those who died in the Hundred Years' War with France. It is unique among Oxford colleges in having no undergraduates other than four 'Bible Clerks'.

It is good to find confirmation of Belloc's lines about the Dons who

. . . sail in amply bellying gown
Enormous through the Sacred Town.

The Cotswold Ridgeway is part of a network of
prehistoric routes that seems to have covered most
of Britain. The early people who lived in these parts
found it much easier to travel on the hilltops and
ridges rather than in the heavily forested and often
marshy valley bottoms. Later settlers preferred the
lower ground which, with their better tools, they
could clear without difficulty. So the Ridgeway runs
close to numerous barrows and other prehistoric
sites, but seems to avoid the villages that grew out of
the later settlements.

One site close to the Ridgeway is the chamber tomb
known as Wayland's Smithy, where travellers may,
according to legend, get their horses shod by leaving
them and a suitable coin there overnight. This
tradition is an ancient one: Wayland, a metalworker
in Norse mythology, is mentioned in connection
with the site in an Anglo-Saxon land charter of
about 955 AD. Near by, at the splendidly named
Snivelling Corner, there used to be a standing stone
thrown by Wayland at his imp, Flibbertigibbet, for
going birds' nesting when sent to fetch nails.

A sturdy cattle shelter at Minster Lovell.

The Great Hall (*opposite*) of Minster Lovell Manor,
built in the fifteenth century. This was the home of
Francis Lovell, Richard III's chief minister, who,
finding himself on the losing side in the Wars of
the Roses, went into hiding in the manor, according
to tradition. Over two hundred years later some
builder's men working on the house accidentally
broke into a secret chamber where they found the
body of a man seated at a table with, beside him, his
dog. Rather less legendary is the Minster Lovell
Jewel, a Saxon piece of gold filigree and enamel,
which was found here.

These curious long narrow mounds, to be seen in many parts of the country as far north as Yorkshire, are a reminder of a method of farming that goes back to Saxon times. A village would farm its land on a communal basis, each farmer being allotted a share of the huge 'open fields'. These shares consisted of one or more plots or strips, not unlike those of a modern allotment, which would probably be dotted haphazardly about the fields. The boundaries between the strips were sometimes marked by stones, but nearly always there were drainage furrows ploughed around the plots to carry away the rain, and it is this 'ridge and furrow' pattern that is still often visible today. The open-field system of farming continued certainly until the seventeenth century, when improvements in agricultural methods began to be introduced which culminated in the industrialisation of farming in the eighteenth century. The enclosure of the old unfenced fields brought sudden distress to many country people who were evicted from land farmed by their ancestors for a thousand years.

A method of ploughing using two traction engines, seldom if ever used 'for real' these days, is sometimes demonstrated at ploughing competitions. One traction engine was stationed at each end of a large field, and first one and then the other would pull across the field a special plough ingeniously designed to work in either direction without being turned round at the end of a run. All that was needed was a great deal of wire cable.

Almost the only known way of hedging nowadays
seems to involve a tractor-borne device like a
gigantic vertical lawnmower. With this it is easy
(only too easy, say some) to slash and rip and hack a
hedge back to look something like a real hedge.
What it does not do is the proper craft of hedging —
that is, constructing an impenetrable barrier out of
living material using only judgement, skill and
patience. Given that, the hedge will last for years;
without it, it will quite soon die. Hedging is not
unlike building a dry-stone wall: both need a feeling
for the material and a neatness of mind that we have
so far failed to build into even the most sophisticated
machinery in the world.

A postmaster's cottage garden.

The great Last Judgement in the west window of Fairford church is often reproduced, but the lesser-known glass is just as fine. The four scenes are Eve and the Serpent, Moses and the burning bush, Gideon and the fleece, and Solomon and Sheba. It dates from about 1500, perhaps the summit of achievement for the English stained glass artists. The whole church is a gem: when visiting it you should on no account miss the superb misericords.

This house at Broughton Poggs (*opposite*) has an unusual fence made of stone slabs set on end.

A fine team competing in a ploughing competition at Burford.

Curious barrel-vaulted tombs at Burford.

A good place for a chat: Arlington Row, Bibury.

Acknowledgements

The photographs were kindly provided by:
John Bethell, St Albans 8-9, 26 top, 56-57, 58-59, 88-89, 92, 93, 95
top, 101 bottom, 102 bottom, 102-103, 104-105, 107 bottom, 112,
113, 114; British Tourist Authority, London 55, 77 top; J. Allan Cash,
London 2, 42 bottom, 53 bottom, 66-67; Bruce Coleman, Uxbridge
83; Clive Coote, London 86; Cotswold Farm Park, Guiting Power
45; W. F. Davidson, Penrith 32 top, 53 top, 59 bottom, 94, 95
bottom, 97 top, 97 bottom; Michael Dent, Richmond 28-29, 29 top,
29 bottom, 31, 32 bottom, 35, 50, 50-51, 51, 70; Greg Evans, London
33; Jack Farley, Gloucester 10-11, 14-15, 36, 37 bottom, 39, 42 top,
46-47, 47, 59 top, 61, 64 bottom, 69, 71 top, 71 bottom, 72-73, 74, 75,
77 bottom, 78-79, 81 top, 90; Marion Farley, Gloucester 68, 76, 78;
Hamlyn Group Picture Library 123; Heart of England Tourist Board,
Worcester 20, 37 top, 80, 81 bottom, 82, 96, 98, 99, 100; John
Howard, Weybridge 18-19, 21, 54 top, 54 bottom, 110-111; Andrew
Lawson, Charlbury 48, 49 top, 49 bottom, 101 top, 102 top, 106, 107
top, 108, 109, 110 top, 111, 115, 116-117, 118, 119, 120-121, 122,
124-125, 125; Mike Roberts, Greenford 62-63, 63; Kenneth Scowen,
Headley Grove 30; Severn Valley Railway—B. S. Moone 87; Tony
Stone Associates, London 18, 22-23, 27, 40-41, 52-53, 84-85, 126-127;
Joyce Teakle, London 38-39, 60; Judy Todd, London 34, 65; Colin
Ward, Laleham 24-25, 36-37, 84, 90-91; Wildfowl Trust,
Slimbridge—J. B. Blossom 64 top; Andy Williams, Guildford 17, 26
bottom, 43, 44.